Mr. Nick's Knitting

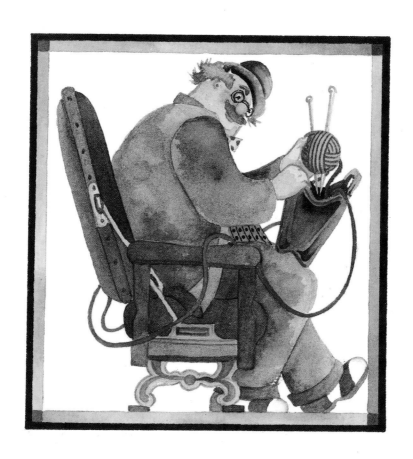

For Gregory

Mr. Nick's Knitting

Written by

Margaret Wild

Illustrated by

Dee Huxley

HARCOURT BRACE & COMPANY · SEVENTY-FIVE YEARS · 1919–1994

A Voyager Book
Harcourt Brace & Company
SAN DIEGO   NEW YORK   LONDON
Printed in Singapore

Every morning on the seven o'clock train to the city Mr. Nick opened his briefcase and took out his knitting.

Mr. Nick loved to knit and so did his friend Mrs. Jolley.

Mrs. Jolley knitted toys like hedgehogs and
kangaroos, monkeys and lions.

Mr. Nick knitted sweaters, big ones and small ones, for his twenty-two nieces and nephews, who grew bigger each year.

Mrs. Jolley helped Mr. Nick when he dropped his stitches and he helped her untangle her yarn. Mrs. Jolley was a very untidy knitter.

While they knitted they looked at the other passengers and stared out the window at the tops of roofs, into small back gardens, and at yachts and ferries in the harbor.

"I love traveling by train," said Mrs. Jolley. "There is always something to see."

Mr. Nick loved knitting and sitting next to Mrs. Jolley. And the other passengers enjoyed listening to the click-clack-click of the needles as Mr. Nick and Mrs. Jolley knitted for forty-five minutes—all the way to the city.

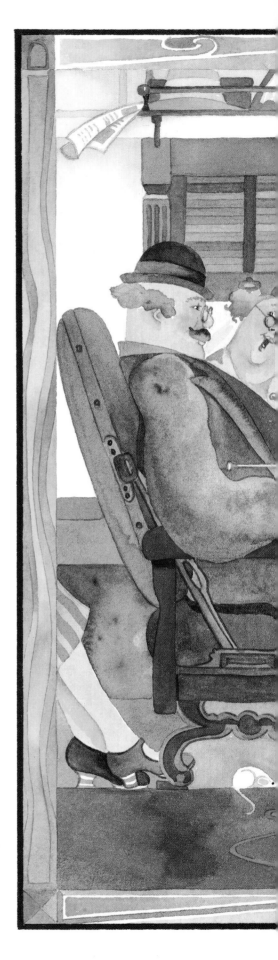

One Monday morning Mrs. Jolley wasn't on the seven o'clock train to the city. Mr. Nick took out his knitting as usual and knitted by himself.

Mrs. Jolley wasn't on the train on Tuesday or on Wednesday either. Mr. Nick dropped three stitches, and there was no one to help him find them. He missed Mrs. Jolley. It was no fun knitting without her beside him.

On Thursday there was a message for Mr. Nick. It said: "Your friend Mrs. Jolley is very ill. She is in the hospital."

That morning Mr. Nick didn't catch the seven o'clock train to the city. Instead he went shopping. He bought Mrs. Jolley a GET WELL card, six balls of beautiful pink wool, and a new pair of knitting needles. Then he went to visit her.

Mrs. Jolley was all alone in a small white bed in a small white room.

"I'm so glad you've come to see me," she said to Mr. Nick. "The doctor says I'm going to be in bed for a long, long time. I miss traveling with you on the train. The nurses are very kind to me, but there's nothing interesting to look at here. Nothing at all."

Mr. Nick gave her the six balls of beautiful pink wool and the new knitting needles. He helped her cast on.

"I think I'll knit a pink elephant," said Mrs. Jolley, and she began to cry. She didn't want to be in the hospital for a long, long time. She missed looking at the other passengers. She missed staring out the window at the tops of roofs, into small back gardens, at yachts and ferries in the harbor.

Mr. Nick helped her untangle her yarn and gave her a big hug.

Then he went home to think of a way to cheer up Mrs. Jolley.

In the morning Mr. Nick caught the seven o'clock train to the city. He opened his briefcase and took out his knitting. But this time he wasn't knitting a sweater for one of his twenty-two nieces and nephews. He was knitting something very special. Something that had lots and lots of small squares.

Mr. Nick knitted nonstop for seven days and seven nights.

He knitted during his lunch hour
and in the bathtub,

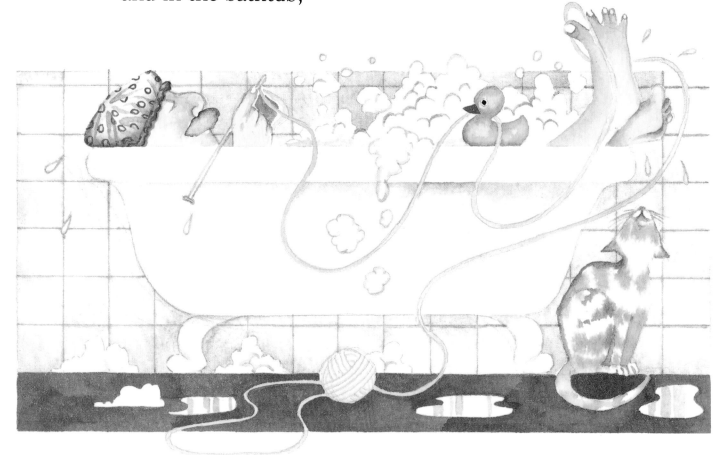

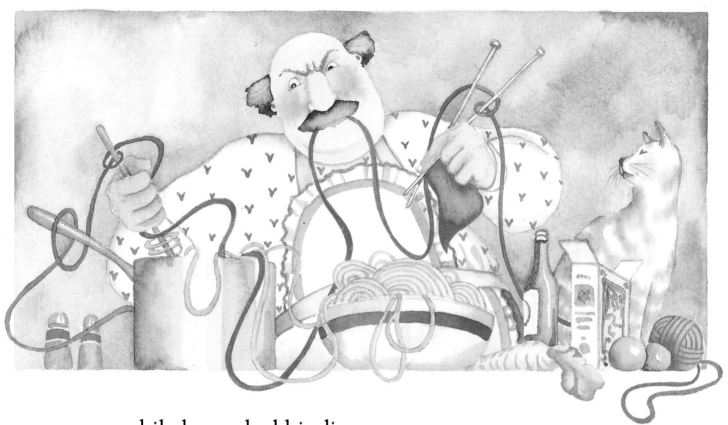

while he cooked his dinner
and while he listened to the radio.

And, of course, he knitted
on the train, click-clack-click,
for forty-five minutes—all the
way to the city.

On the eighth day Mr. Nick
sewed all the squares together
and went to visit Mrs. Jolley
in the hospital.

Mrs. Jolley looked very sad and lonely in her small white bed in the small white room.

"I'm so glad you've come to see me," said Mrs. Jolley. "Tell me what's been happening on the train. What did you see out the window? There's nothing interesting to look at here—nothing at all."

Mr. Nick gently placed his big package on the bed and helped her unwrap it.

Mrs. Jolley didn't say anything for a moment.
Then she burst into tears and said, "I'm so
happy! This is the best present anyone has
ever given me.

"Now I'll always have something interesting to look at, even if I have to stay in the hospital for a long, long time." She gave Mr. Nick a big hug.

The next morning on the seven o'clock train to the city Mr. Nick opened his briefcase and took out his knitting. He was knitting a sweater for one of his *twenty-three* nieces and nephews, who grew bigger each year.

And the same morning at seven o'clock in the hospital, Mrs. Jolley took out her knitting. While she knitted she looked at the passengers and stared at the tops of roofs, into small back gardens, and at yachts and ferries in the harbor.

Click-clack-click went Mr. Nick's and Mrs. Jolley's needles as they knitted happily for forty-five minutes—all the way to the city.

First published 1988 by Hodder & Stoughton
(Australia) Pty Limited

Text copyright © 1988 by Margaret Wild
Illustrations copyright © 1988 by Dee Huxley

First U. S. edition 1989

Requests for permission to make copies of any
part of the work should be mailed to:
Permissions Department,
Harcourt Brace & Company, 6277 Sea Harbor Drive,
Orlando, Florida 32887-6777.

Library of Congress Cataloging-in-Publication Data
Wild, Margaret, 1948–
Mr. Nick's knitting.
Summary: Feeling lonely when he discovers his
knitting partner Mrs. Jolly is in the hospital,
Mr. Nick knits a very special gift to cheer up his friend.
[1.Knitting—Fiction. 2. Friendship—Fiction]
I. Huxley, Dee. II. Title.
PZ7.W64574Mr 1989   [E]   88-35778
ISBN 0-15-200518-8
ISBN 0-15-200116-6 (pbk.)

A B C D E
A B C D E (pbk.)

Printed in Singapore